William S. (William Scudder) Stryker

The New Jersey Volunteers

Loyalists in the Revolutionary War

William S. (William Scudder) Stryker

The New Jersey Volunteers
Loyalists in the Revolutionary War

ISBN/EAN: 9783744659376

Printed in Europe, USA, Canada, Australia, Japan

Cover: Foto ©ninafisch / pixelio.de

More available books at **www.hansebooks.com**

THE NEW JERSEY VOLUNTEERS"

(LOYALISTS)

N THE REVOLUTIONARY WAR.

BY

WILLIAM S. STRYKER,

ADJUTANT-GENERAL OF NEW JERSEY.

PRINTED FOR PRIVATE DISTRIBUTION.

TRENTON, N. J.

NAAR, DAY & NAAR, BOOK AND JOB PRINTERS.

1887.

THE NEW JERSEY VOLUNTEERS--LOYALISTS--
IN THE REVOLUTIONARY WAR.

The facts contained in this paper in reference to the Loyalists of New Jersey in the military service of the Crown during the Revolutionary war, are principally compiled from Force's American Archives, O'Callaghan's Documentary History of New York, Gaines' Register, Howe's Narrative, Galloway's Pamphlets, Moore's Diary of the American Revolution, Dawson's Historical Magazine, Hatfield's History of Elizabeth, Whitehead's History of Perth Amboy, Minutes of the Provincial Congress and Council of Safety of New Jersey, Sparks' Writings of Washington, Simcoe's Military Journal, Greene's Life of General Greene, Pennsylvania Archives—first and second series, Lossing's Field-book of the Revolution, Tarleton's Southern Campaigns, Sir Henry Clinton's Narrative, Draper's Kings' Mountain, Dawson's Battles by Land and Sea, Barber & Howe's New Jersey Historical Collections, New York Journal, Rivington's Gazette, Ramsey's South Carolina, Sims' South Carolina, and the records on file in my office. But, of course, Sabine's Loyalists of the American Revolution has been constantly consulted; without it this sketch could certainly not have been written.

As soon as General William Howe arrived at Staten Island, on the 7th of July, 1776, so pleased was he with his reception in the harbour of New York that he wrote these words to the British government: "I have great reason to expect an enormous body of the inhabitants to join the army from the provinces of York, the Jerseys and Connecticut, who, in this time of universal oppression, only wait for opportunities to give proofs of their loyalty and zeal for government. Sixty men came over two days ago with a few arms from the neighbourhood of Shrewsbury, in Jersey, who were desirous to serve, and I understand there are five hundred more in that quarter ready to follow their example."

General Howe soon after this began to appoint recruiting officers in different parts of New Jersey and to organize detachments of Provincials as fast as they presented themselves for service in the army. Mr. Cortlandt Skinner, whose devotion to the interests of the British king before the war had made him a prominent man in New Jersey, was selected as the proper officer to organize and to command the men who were anxious to enroll themselves under the standard of Great Britain. He was commissioned at first a Colonel, and afterwards a Brigadier-General, with authority to raise five battalions to consist of two thousand and five hundred soldiers, "under command of gentlemen of the country nominated by himself." He established his headquarters at the organization of the corps on Staten Island, in New York harbour, and this place soon became the refuge for all tories of New York and New Jersey, as well as for deserters from the patriot army. General Skinner himself seems to have been stationed on Staten Island and in New York city during most of the war, and it is very seldom that we meet him even with his soldiers in any other part of the contiguous country. We learn from General Howe's Narrative that at the beginning of the campaign of 1777 General Skinner had been able to recruit but five hundred and seventeen men of his complement, but in November, 1777, he had eight hundred and fifty-nine men on his brigade rolls, and in May, 1778, "after several months of active exertions," he had enlisted one thousand one hundred and one men. But at that time the nucleus for six battalions had been made and the officers commissioned. During that year five hundred and fifty additional volunteers, mostly from New Jersey, were enrolled for service, and afterward sent to Charleston, South Carolina. It is then apparent that General Skinner recruited about two-thirds of the quota first assigned to him. All of these soldiers immediately on enlistment were placed in active service, and they began to distinguish themselves at an early day in their great zeal to annoy, intimidate and injure their former patriot friends and neighbours.

In a letter written by General Howe to Lord George Germain, dated New York, December 20th, 1776, this remark is made: "I cannot close this letter without making mention of the good service rendered in the course of the campaign by Cortlandt Skinner, Esq., Attorney-General in the Jerseys, who has been indefatigable and of infinite service since the army entered those provinces. I therefore humbly recommend him as a gentleman meriting royal favour." Thus early was General Skinner showing his devotion to the King. This was just after the retreat of Washington's army through New Jersey, and General Skinner was urging his own friends to take protection from the British. It was also just prior to what was called "the unfortunate affair" at Trenton.

In Brasher's Journal, February, 1777, appears the following new catechism :

Q. " Who is the most ungrateful man in the world ? "

A. " Governor Skinner."

Q. " Why do you call him Governor ? "

A. " Because when Lord and General Howe thought that they had conquered the Jerseys they appointed him Lieutenant Governor of that State. Skinner assumed that title over one-tenth part of the said State and continued his usurpation for six weeks, five days, thirty-six minutes, ten seconds and thirty-one hundredth parts of a second and was then deposed."

Q. " Why is he called ungrateful ? "

A. " Because he has joined the enemies of his country and enlisted men to fight against his neighbours, his friends and his kinsfolk ; because he has endeavoured to transfer the soil that gave him bread from the rightful possessors to a foreign hand ; and because, to gain present ease and transitory honours, he would fasten the chains of slavery on three millions of people and their offspring forever."

The answers to these questions clearly show the opinion which patriotic Jerseymen held of General Skinner and of the efforts which he had already made to restore them to their allegiance to England.

In Rivington's Army List of 1778, as found in the Historical Society of Pennsylvania, we find the first complete roster of the officers of the six battalions of the New Jersey Volunteers. This probably shows the state of the organization in the early part of summer of that year. The compilation has been carefully made, the spelling of the names corrected, and it is now set forth in proper official style.

Brigadier-General,   . . . Cortlandt Skinner.
Chaplain, ... Edward Winslow.

FIRST BATTALION.

Lieutenant-Colonel,   . . Elisha Lawrence.
Major, ... Thomas Leonard.
Adjutant,   .   . . Patrick Henry.
Quartermaster,   . James Nealson.
Surgeon, ... William Peterson.
Captains, ... John Barbarie,
                          John Longstreet,
                          Garret Keating,
                          Richard Cayford.
Captain-Lieutenant,   . James Nealson.
Lieutenants,   . . . John Taylor,
                          Thomas Oakason,
                          Samuel Leonard,
                          John Throckmorton,
                          John Monro,
                          Patrick Henry,
                          Robert Peterson.
Ensigns,   . John Robbins,
                          John Thompson,
                          Richard Lippincott,
                          William Lawrence,
                          Hector McLean.

SECOND BATTALION.

Lieutenant-Colonel,   . . . John Morris.
First Major, ... John Antill.
Second Major, ... John Colden.
Adjutant, ... Thomas T. Pritchard.
Quartermaster,   . Thomas Morrison.
Surgeon, ... Charles Earle.
Surgeon's Mate, ... James Boggs.
Chaplain, ... John Rowland.
Captains, ... Donald Campbell,
                          George Stanforth,

Captains, . .	. Waldron Bleau,
	Norman McLeod,
	Cornelius McLeod,
	Uriah Bleau.
Lieutenants,	John DeMonzes,
	Thomas T. Pritchard,
	William VanDumont,
	Josiah Parker,
	William Stevenson.
Ensigns,	. William K. Hurlet,
	Thomas Morrison.

THIRD BATTALION.

First Major,	. Robert Drummond.
Second Major,	. Philip VanCortlandt.
Adjutant, . .	. John Jenkins.
Quartermaster.	. John Falker.
Surgeon, .	. Henry Dongan.
Captains, .	. John Hatfield,
	Samuel Hudnot,
	David Alston.
Captain-Lieutenant.	. John Alston.
Lieutenants, .	. Anthony Hollinshead,
	John Jenkins,
	John Troup,
	William Chew,
	Francis Frazer.
Ensigns,	. James Brasier LeGrange,
	John Camp,
	John Willis,
	Jonathan Alston.

FOURTH BATTALION.

Lieutenant-Colonel,	. Abraham Van Buskirk.
First Major, . .	Daniel Isaac Browne.
Second Major,	. Robert Timpany.
Adjutant, . .	. Arthur Maddox.
Quartermaster,	. William Sorrell.

Surgeon, ... John Hammell.
Captains, ... William Van Allen,
                      Samuel Heyden,
                      Peter Ruttan,
                      Patrick Campbell,
                      Daniel Bessonet,
                      Samuel Ryerson,
                      Arthur Maddox.
Lieutenants,   . . . Edward Earle,
                      Martin Ryerson,
                      John Van Buskirk,
                      Michael Smith,
                      James Servanier,
                      Donald McPherson,
                      John Hyslop.
Ensigns,   . . John Simonson,
                      James Cole,
                      Justus Earle,
                      John Van Norden,
                      Colin McVane,
                      George Ryerson.

FIFTH BATTALION.

Lieutenant-Colonel, . . . Joseph Barton.
Major, ... Thomas Millidge.
Adjutant, ... Isaac Hedden.
Quartermaster, ... Fleming Colgan.
Surgeon, ... Uzal Johnson.
Surgeon's Mate, ... Stephen Millidge.
Captains, ... Joseph Crowell,
                      James Shaw,
                      Benjamin Barton,
                      John Williams.
Lieutenants, ... John Cougle,
                      Isaac Hedden,
                      Joseph Waller,
                      William Hutchinson,
                      Christopher Insley,
                      Daniel Shannon,

Lieutenants, ... John Reid.
Ensigns, ... Patrick Haggerty.
Ezekiel Dennis,
Peter Anderson,
Joseph Bean.

SIXTH BATTALION.

Lieutenant-Colonel, . . Isaac Allen.
Major, . . . Richard V. Stockton.
Captains, . . Joseph Lee,
Peter Campbell,
Charles Harrison.
Lieutenants, . John Vought,
John Hatton,
Edward Steele.
Ensigns, . Daniel Grandin,
Cornelius Thompson,
James Service.

Some mention must be made of the skirmishes of detachments of the Militia of New Jersey and of the Continental Line with "Skinner's Greens," as they were called, whenever those loyalists left Staten Island for a tour of plunder on the rich fields of New Jersey, and note must also be made of direct attacks on the tory forces on Staten Island, as well as a brief statement of the conduct of those loyal battalions in their campaign in the South.

On the morning of February 18th, 1777, Colonel John Neilson, of the Second Regiment, Middlesex county, New Jersey Militia, with a small detachment of his command, captured Major Richard V. Stockton, of the Sixth Battalion of the Volunteers, with fifty-nine enlisted men, on Lawrence Island. Four men were killed in the skirmish, their arms were taken and some camp equipage.

During the spring and summer of 1777, the New Jersey

Volunteers made various excursions into New Jersey for forage for the British army. This became so annoying that Colonel Matthias Ogden, of the First Battalion, New Jersey Continental Line, then commanding the post at Elizabeth Town, with Colonel Elias Dayton, of the Third Battalion, who was stationed at Newark, and a party of one hundred militia of Essex county, determined to inflict some severe punishment on Skinner's tories. On the 22d of August they were re-enforced by a thousand men of the brigade of Brigadier-General William Smallwood, of Maryland, and of Brigadier-General Chevalier Preudhomme DeBorro, and just before midnight they crossed over from Halstead's Point, near the mouth of Morse's creek, to Staten Island. The New Jersey Volunteers were then stationed from Decker's Ferry to Billops's, now Ward's Point. The attack by the Jersey Continentals, before daylight the next morning, resulted in taking prisoner Lieutenant-Colonel Elisha Lawrence, of the First Battalion, and Lieutenant-Colonel Joseph Barton, of the Fifth Battalion of the Volunteers, with one hundred and thirty enlisted men of their commands, and in severely wounding Major John Barnes, of the First Battalion, and Lieutenant-Colonel Edward Vaughan Dongan, of the Third Battalion, from which wounds they both died. General Sullivan, however, with the other body of Continentals, endeavored at the same time to surprise the Volunteers, but was deceived by a tory guide, and having come upon the loyal troops awaiting him, was quite severely punished by them. Indeed, General Skinner claimed the affair, notwithstanding his loss, as a great victory.

On the 27th of November, 1777, General Philemon Dickinson, commanding officer of the New Jersey Militia, suddenly embarked before daylight from Halstead's Point to

Staten Island with a party of about fourteen hundred militia. He advanced his men in three different detachments by different roads, to rendezvous at a central point seven miles distant. Unfortunately, it was soon found that General Skinner had been informed of the intended attack, and before three o'clock he had drawn his troops off the island. General Dickinson, however, made a few little attacks on some straggling parties of the tories and on the detachment of the British troops under Major-General John Campbell, and he killed some five or six men and took twenty-four prisoners. He lost three men of his command captured, and two wounded. The main object designed by this affair was not accomplished, but General Washington was pleased with the disposal made of the forces by General Dickinson and the manner in which they had been handled.

A considerable body of the New Jersey Volunteers spent the winter of 1777–'78 in the gay life which the British soldiery enjoyed during that season in Philadelphia. The rest of the force remained on Staten Island. From Howe's Narrative we find that during their occupancy of Philadelphia the British held out special inducements for men to enlist in the loyal corps, but they were obliged to report that they obtained but "three troops of light dragoons, consisting of one hundred and thirty-two troopers and one hundred and seventy-four real volunteers, from Jersey, under Colonel Vandyke." The service of this officer, whether he was a Jerseyman or a resident of Pennsylvania, has not been ascertained, nor can it be said what became of the "real volunteers" and what military duties they performed.

On April 2d, 1778, a detachment of New Jersey Volunteers left Philadelphia for the purpose of garrisoning the fort at Billingsport, New Jersey. A small attack was made by the militia of New Jersey from Elizabeth Town Port at one o'clock on the morning of June 9th, 1778, and they effected a landing on Staten Island and fired upon the Provincial troops that were still stationed there. Again, just before daylight, they attempted to land in ten boats, said to contain one hundred men, but they were greeted with a quick discharge of firearms and were driven back. It is thus seen that the tories were not left entirely undisturbed in possession of this beautiful garden island.

On the evening of June 12th, 1778, Captain Cornelius Hatfield, Jr., of the Jersey Volunteers, crossed over the sound and plundered the residence of Lieutenant John Haviland, of the First Regiment of Essex county, New Jersey, Militia, and carried him off a prisoner.

Some portion of the New Jersey Volunteers crossed the State from Cooper's Point to Sandy Hook, with General Sir Henry Clinton, in his memorable march through New Jersey, in June, 1778.

After the battle of Monmouth, June 28th, 1778, General Washington posted at Elizabeth Town the Brigade of Jersey Continentals under General William Maxwell to guard and keep in check the armed tories on Staten Island.

On the 15th day of October, 1778, Captain Patrick Ferguson, of the Seventieth Regiment British Foot, with a detachment of the Third New Jersey Volunteers, made a descent on Little Neck, New Jersey, on Egg Harbour Inlet, surprised a detachment of Count Pulaski's troops and killed some fifty of his men.

On the 27th day of November, 1778, an expedition with two thousand troops sailed from Sandy Hook for Savannah, Georgia, and six days after landing at Tybee Island, off the harbour of that city, they took part in the fight, December 29th, on Brewton Hill. A detachment of the New Jersey Volunteers, Lieutenant-Colonel Allen commanding, went out with this party and suffered considerably in the battle just mentioned. Captain Peter Campbell, one of the most gallant officers of the detachment, was killed.

In the year 1779 the brigade of New Jersey Volunteers was so far consolidated, as to reduce the organization to four battalions. A number of the officers were retired and the roster of the force appeared as follows, as we find from McDonald & Cameron's List, in the Royal Institution of London:

Brigadier-General. .	. Cortlandt Skinner.
Chaplain, .	. Edward Winslow.

FIRST BATTALION.

Lieutenant-Colonel,	. Joseph Barton.
Major, . . .	. Thomas Millidge.
Adjutant, . .	. Isaac Hedden.
Quartermaster,	. Bartholomew Doughty.
Surgeon,	. Uzal Johnson.
Captains, .	. Joseph Crowell.
	Garret Keating,
	James Shaw,
	Richard Cayford,
	John Cougle.
Lieutenants,	. James Nealson,
	Joseph Cunliff,
	Patrick Haggerty.
	Isaac Hedden,
	Samuel Leonard,
	William Hutchinson,
	John Taylor.
Ensigns,	. John Lawrence,
	James Brittain,

Ensigns, ... Zenophon Jewett,
                          John Thompson,
                          John Reid,
                          William Lawrence,
                          James Moody.

SECOND BATTALION.

Lieutenant-Colonel, . . . John Morris.
First Major, ... John Antill.
Second Major, ... John Colden.
Adjutant, ... Thomas T. Pritchard.
Quartermaster, ... Thomas Morrison.
Surgeon, ... Charles Earle.
Chaplain, ... John Rowland.
Captains, ... Waldron Bleau,
                          Cornelius McLeod,
                          Donald Campbell,
                          George Stanforth.
Lieutenants, ... John DeMonzes,
                          William Van Dumont,
                          Thomas T. Pritchard,
                          Josiah Parker,
                          Thomas Morrison,
                          Charles Babbington,
                          George Lambert,
                          Samuel Richard Wilson,
                          William Stevenson.
Ensigns, . Uriah Bleau,
                          James Brasier LeGrange.

THIRD BATTALION.

Lieutenant-Colonel, . . . Isaac Allen.
Major, ... Robert Drummond.
Adjutant, ... John Jenkins.
Quartermaster, . . . John Falker.
Surgeon, ... William Peterson.
Chaplain, ... Thomas Barton.

Captains, . .   . Joseph Lee,
                          Patrick Campbell,
                          Samuel Hudnot,
                          Charles Harrison,
                          Bartholomew Thatcher,
                          Daniel Cozens,
                          Thomas Hunlock.
Lieutenants,   . Edward Steele,
                          John Hatton,
                          John Troup,
                          William Chew,
                          James Harrison,
                          John Coombes,
                          John Jenkins,
                          Enoch Lyon,
                          William Turner.
Ensigns,   . John Willis,
                          John Camp,
                          Cornelius Thompson,
                          Nathaniel Coombes,
                          Jonathan Alston,
                          Peter Dunworth,
                          John Seamon,
                          Richard McGinnis,
                          George Swanton.

FOURTH BATTALION.

Lieutenant-Colonel,   . . Abraham Van Buskirk.
Major, .   . Philip Van Cortlandt.
Adjutant,   . . ——— ———.
Surgeon,   . John Hammell.
Chaplain,   . Daniel Batwell.
Captains, .   . William Van Allen,
                          Peter Ruttan,
                          Samuel Ryerson.
Lieutenants,   . Edward Earle,
                          Martin Ryerson,
                          John Van Buskirk,

Lieutenants, ... James Servanier,
John Hyslop.
Ensigns, . John Simonson,
John Van Norden,
Justus Earle,
Colin McVane,
James Cole.

During the year 1779 General Skinner offered a reward of 2,000 guineas for the capture of Governor Livingston, of New Jersey, dead or alive. This excited the cupidity and the reckless zeal of many of the Jersey loyalists. A very spicy correspondence ensued in March and April, 1779, between the Governor and Sir Henry Clinton in reference to this attempted exploit. In May, 1780, we find Ensign James Moody, of the First Battalion, whose very name was a terror to patriots in New Jersey, leading an expedition for the seizure of the Governor.

On the 10th of May, 1779, about one hundred men of the Third Battalion, New Jersey Volunteers, crossing from New York city by way of New Dock, attacked their old Bergen county neighbors at Closter. They killed Cornelius Demarest and wounded three other farmers and burned the dwelling houses and barns of seven of the inhabitants of the village. The militia in that part of the county in the companies of Captains Abraham J. Blauvelt, Cornelius Harring and John Huyler immediately gathered and pursued the tory bands. The Loyalists succeeded, however, in carrying off four of the patriots, but obtained no cattle, no forage, or any plunder of any kind.

During the summer of 1779 a considerable detachment of the New Jersey Volunteers was sent to reinforce the British army in South Carolina, and took part in the

2

assault on Savannah, October 9th, 1779. A battalion under command of Lieutenant-Colonel Isaac Allen formed part of the garrison of one of the large redoubts on the south side of the city, near the river. Captain Daniel Cozens, of the Third Battalion, lost his life in this engagement.

On the 9th of January, 1780, Brigadier-General William Irvine received orders from General Washington to ascertain the situation and strength of General Skinner's Brigade on Staten Island. The night of the 14th of January was selected for the enterprise, and Major-General Lord Stirling was detailed to command the forces, which moved in three distinct detachments. The party started on the morning of the 15th, crossed the ice on sleds from DeHart's Point to Staten Island, and one detachment marched towards Dongan's Mills, another toward what is now Tompkinsville, and the third detachment toward Decker's Ferry. The tories, again apprised of their coming, were found strongly guarded in their works, and it was with some difficulty and address that Lord Stirling was able to withdraw his command in safety, not even daring to attack them in their intrenchments. He had learned that a channel had been opened in the ice from New York, and that large re-enforcements were on their way from that city.

A party of New Jersey Volunteers of the First and Third Battalions—in all one hundred and thirty-two men—under Lieutenant Van Buskirk, with twelve British dragoons under command of Lieutenant Stuart, made a raid on Elizabeth Town on the evening of January 25th, 1780, and carried off five officers and forty-seven soldiers. They also burned the Presbyterian Church, the Court House and the School House. Captain Cornelius Hatfield, Jr., was the guide of the tory troops on this occasion, and the incendiary work was ascribed to the discredit of this malicious man, whose father was, at that very time, an elder in the church destroyed by his wanton conduct.

On the evening of February 10th, 1780, the British and tory troops on Staten Island made another raid on Elizabeth Town, plundering the residences of many prominent citizens and made active search for Judge Elisha Boudinot and the Honorable William Peartree Smith, both noted patriots.

On March 24th, 1780, they tried the same experiment, and this time took Major Matthias Halsted a prisoner.

On June 7th, 1780, two battalions of the New Jersey Volunteers having been assigned to the division commanded by the Hessian General Knyphausen, crossed over to Elizabeth Town, marched as far as Connecticut Farms and thence to Springfield, New Jersey. In the battle of Springfield, which was fought June 23d, 1780, these two battalions marched on either flank of the division of Major-General Matthews, and on the march and during the fight exchanged many shots with the patriot troops.

In the forces commanded by Lieutenant-Colonel Patrick Ferguson, and generally spoken of as British regulars, a considerable number of picked men of the New Jersey Volunteers had been assigned for special service. Captain Patrick Campbell of the Second Battalion, commanded the detachment of light infantry which belonged to the command of Colonel Alexander Innes. This corps took an active part in the fight at King's Mountain, South Carolina, October 7th, 1780. Captains Patrick Campbell and Samuel Ryerson were wounded and Ensign Richard McGinnis was killed in this fight.

On the evening of November 4th, 1780, a party of the

Volunteers came over from Staten Island to Elizabeth Town, and on this occasion captured Colonel Matthias Ogden, of the First Regiment, Jersey Continental Line, and Captain Jonathan Dayton of the Third Regiment. Enterprises of this kind were frequent during the winter of 1780–'81. Especially was this so on March 21st, 26th and 27th and June 26th, 1781.

In the siege of Fort Ninety-Six in South Carolina, May 22d, 1781, the garrison consisted partly of men of the Second Battalion of the Volunteers. Captain Patrick Campbell commanded a party of thirty men, who, at one stage of the siege, made a sally from the rear of the battery and fell on the flank of the American troops and a desperate contest ensued. Captain John Barbarie and Lieutenant John Hatton were badly wounded. The New Jersey Volunteers took part also in the fight at Guilford, at Cowpens, at Eutaw Springs, and at the siege of Charleston. At the battle of Eutaw Springs, Captain James Shaw, of the First Battalion, was mortally wounded and died soon afterward, and Captain John Barbarie, of the same organization, Captain Jacob Van Buskirk and Lieutenant John Troup, of the Third Battalion, received serious wounds.

On September 4th, 1781, the Fourth Battalion left New York with Arnold's expedition for the attack on New London, Connecticut. They landed near that village on September 6th, meditating only plunder and not battle. The battalion took part in the closing scene of the desperate defence of Fort Griswold, and the murder of Lieutenant-Colonel William Ledyard, after he had given up his sword, is often in history given to the discredit of Lieutenant-Colonel Van Buskirk. This certainly, however, is an error. General Arnold detached the Fourth Battalion under com-

mand of Lieutenant-Colonel Joshua Upham, of Massachusetts, to take a hill which commanded the village.
This was very quickly done, and General Arnold followed
the force to the hill, which had been taken. During this
fight they were compelled to storm Groton Fort. They
massacred the garrison and burned the village of New
London.

Among the "prisoners taken in the garrisons of York
and Gloucester, October 19th, 1781," we find that there was
a captain, a lieutenant and two enlisted men of the Third
Regiment, New Jersey Volunteers. This little party evidently failed to escape on the transport vessels to New York,
on which Lord Cornwallis had placed all the Loyalists who
had taken part in the siege of Yorktown.

In Gaines' Register for 1782, in the Historical Society of
Pennsylvania, we find a roster of the officers of the Volunteers as they appeared by the rolls of that brigade at the
beginning of that year. Lieutenant-Colonel DeLancey had
returned from captivity and many other changes had taken
place in the lists of the officers of Skinner's brigade. The
roster is as follows :

Brigadier-General,   . . . Cortlandt Skinner.

FIRST BATTALION.

Lieutenant-Colonel,   . Stephen DeLancey.
Major, ... Thomas Millidge.
Adjutant, ... Ozias Insley.
Quartermaster, ... John Waddington (Died).
Quartermaster, ... Theodore Valleau.
Surgeon, ... Uzal Johnson,
Chaplain, ... Charles Inglis.
Captains, ... John Colden,
                          Joseph Crowell,

Captains,	John Cougle,
	John Taylor,
	Samuel Leonard.
Captain-Lieutenant,	William Hutchinson.
Lieutenants, . .	Joseph Cunliff,
	Isaac Hedden,
	Patrick Haggerty,
	John Thompson,
	John Lawrence,
	James Moody,
	John Reid,
	William Van Dumont.
Ensigns,	James Brittain,
	Zenophon Jewett,
	Ozias Insley,
	Henry Barton,
	Phineas Millidge,
	John Woodward,
	James Barton,
	Reuben Hankinson,
	Philip Skinner.

SECOND BATTALION.

Lieutenant-Colonel,	Isaac Allen
Major, .	Robert Drummond.
Adjutant, ...	Cornelius Thompson.
Quartermaster,	John Falker.
Surgeon, . .	William Peterson.
Chaplain, .	Charles Morgan.
Captains, .	Joseph Lee,
	Patrick Campbell,
	Charles Harrison,
	Bartholomew Thatcher,
	Daniel Cozens,
	Thomas Hunlock,
	John Barbarie.
Captain-Lieutenant,	Edward Steele.
Lieutenants, ...	John Jenkins,
	William Chew,

Lieutenants, ... John Hatton,
James Harrison,
John Coombes,
Enoch Lyon.

Ensigns, ... John Willis,
Cornelius Thompson,
Nathaniel Coombes,
John Swanton,
John Shannon,
John Leonard,
Lewis Thompson,
George Lee.

THIRD BATTALION.

Lieutenant-Colonel,   . Abraham Van Buskirk.
Major, ... Philip Van Cortlandt.
Adjutant, ... John Hyslop.
Quartermaster,   . William Sorrell.
Surgeon, ... John Hammell.
Surgeon's Mate,   . . ———— Haulenbeck.
Chaplain, ... Daniel Batwell.
Captains, ... William Van Allen,
Peter Ruttan,
Samuel Ryerson,
Jacob Van Buskirk,
Edward Earle,
Waldron Bleau,
Donald Campbell,
Norman McLeod.

Lieutenants.   . . . . . . John Van Buskirk,
James Servanier,
John Hyslop,
John Simonson,
John Van Norden,
Josiah Parker,
William Stevenson,
George Lambert,
Justus Earle.

Ensigns, ... Philip Van Cortlandt, Jr.,
                          William Sorrell,
                          Richard Cooper,
                          John Jewett,
                          Uriah Bleau,
                          Henry Van Allen,
                          Robert Woodward,
                          Stephen Ryder,
                          ——— Hendorff.

A roster of officers of the brigade in 1783, the close of
the war, is given in Rivington's Army List, in the collections of the New York Historical Society. This record was
made about the time the loyalists had abandoned all hope
of sustaining the British power in the new republic, and
were beginning to think where they should flee to escape
the hatred of their former friends and neighbours. The
list is here given :

Brigadier-General, ... Cortlandt Skinner.

FIRST BATTALION.

Lieutenant-Colonel,   . Stephen DeLancey.
Major, ... Thomas Millidge.
Adjutant, ... John Atchison.
Quartermaster,   . ——— ———.
Surgeon, ... Charles Earle.
Chaplain, .   . Charles Inglis.
Captains,   . . . Joseph Crowell,
                         John Cougle,
                         John Taylor,
                         Samuel Leonard,
                         Alexander McDonald,
                         Patrick Haggerty,
                         William Hutchinson.
Captain-Lieutenant, . . . Joseph Cunliff.

Lieutenants,	. . . . Isaac Hedden,
	John Thompson,
	John Lawrence,
	William Van Dumont,
	James Moody,
	John Reid,
	Andrew Stockton,
	James Brittain,
	Henry Barton.
Ensigns, .	. . Zenophon Jewett,
	Ozias Insley,
	Phineas Millidge,
	John Woodward,
	James Barton,
	Reuben Hankinson,
	Philip Skinner,
	John Atchison,
	Joseph Brittain.

SECOND BATTALION.

Lieutenant-Colonel,	. Isaac Allen.
Major, . .	. . Robert Drummond.
Adjutant, ...	. . Cornelius Thompson (Resigned).
Adjutant, ...	. . George Cypher.
Quartermaster,	. . William Falker (Resigned).
Quartermaster,	. Daniel James.
Surgeon, . .	. . Daniel Bancroft.
Chaplain, .	. Charles Morgan (Removed).
Chaplain,	. . James Sayre.
Captains,	Joseph Lee,
	Patrick Campbell,
	Charles Harrison,
	Bartholomew Thatcher,
	Daniel Cozens,
	Thomas Hunlock,
	John Barbarie.
Captain-Lieutenant, .	. Edward Steele.
Lieutenants, ...	. John Jenkins,
	William Turner,

Lieutenants, ... John Hatton,
James Harrison,
John Coombes,
Enoch Lyon,
John Willis,
Cornelius Thompson.

Ensigns. . Nathaniel Coombes,
John Shannon,
William Banks,
John Leonard,
Lewis Thompson,
George Lee,
Ruloff Ruloffs,
Stephen Millidge.

THIRD BATTALION.

Lieutenant-Colonel, . . Abraham Van Buskirk.
Major, . . . Philip Van Cortlandt.
Adjutant, . . John Hyslop.
Quartermaster, . William Sorrell.
Surgeon, . . John Hammell.
Chaplain, . Daniel Batwell.
Captains, . William Van Allen,
Samuel Ryerson,
Jacob Van Buskirk,
Edward Earle,
Waldron Bleau,
Norman McLeod,
Donald Campbell.

Lieutenants, . John Van Buskirk,
James Servanier,
John Hyslop,
John Simonson,
William Stevenson,
Josiah Parker,
George Lambert,
Justus Earle,
Richard Cooper.

Ensigns, . . Philip Van Cortlandt, Jr.,

Ensigns, ... William Sorrell,
John Jewett,
Uriah Bleau,
Henry Van Allen,
Robert Woodward,
Stephen Ryder,
———— Hendorff,
Malcom Wilmott.

In addition to what has been written in reference to the conduct of these tory volunteers during the Revolutionary War, special mention must now be given of the officers who commanded this contingent during that period.

BRIGADIER-GENERAL.

CORTLANDT SKINNER.—A few purely personal facts with regard to General Skinner need only now be added. He was of Scotch ancestry and was born in 1728, was the Speaker of the Colonial Legislature after 1765 and the last Attorney-General of the King for the Province of New Jersey. He was considered a lawyer of marked ability and strict integrity of character. He continued his allegiance to the Crown and received authority to form a corps of loyalists for duty as a brigade of New Jersey Volunteers in the military service. He was made colonel thereof July 1st, 1776, and afterward commissioned brigadier-general. He served as such during the whole war. His family lived in New York city and afterward at Jamaica, Long Island, during the war, and at its conclusion they all sailed for England. He continued through life on the half-pay list of the British Government as a general officer, and he died at Bristol, March 15th, 1799. He married, in 1752, Eliza-

beth, daughter of Philip Kearney, of Perth Amboy, New
Jersey. He had five sons and eleven daughters.

LIEUTENANT-COLONELS.

ISAAC ALLEN.—About the time of General Howe's occu-
pation of Trenton, in December, 1776, the family of Isaac
Allen left their home in that city, accepted protection
papers and were ever afterward considered subjects of King
George. Isaac Allen was commissioned December 3d, 1776,
in the Sixth Battalion. At the siege of Savannah, Georgia,
October 9th, 1779, he appears as in command of the Third
Battalion, but in the later years of the war in the Second
Battalion as its lieutenant-colonel. During the war all
his property in Trenton was confiscated. In the year 1783
he resumed his profession as a lawyer in St. John, New
Brunswick, and in after years took a seat upon the supreme
bench and was a member of the Council of the Province.
His death occurred in the year 1806, in the sixty-fifth year
of his age.

JOSEPH BARTON.—This officer appears on the rolls of
1778 as in command as lieutenant-colonel of the Fifth
Battalion, and, in the following year, of the First Battalion.
He was captured by the patriots under Generals Stirling
and Sullivan, on Staten Island, August 22d, 1777. He left
the service in 1781. Very little is known of his personal
history.

STEPHEN DELANCEY.—He was of the illustrious family
of that name in New York. It does not appear why he
accepted a commission in a New Jersey Regiment as lieu-

tenant-colonel of the First Battalion, but he was commissioned as such September 5th, 1776, while he was a prisoner. On the evening of June 4th, 1776, he was celebrating the birthday of George III, and being loud in his expressions of loyalty, he and his party were arrested by the patriotic citizens of Albany and given in the safe-keeping of Governor Trumbull of Connecticut, who seems to have taken charge during the war of such tories. After his release he was again commissioned lieutenant-colonel of the First Battalion, New Jersey Volunteers, December 25th, 1781, and so continued until the close of the war. After peace was declared he removed to Nova Scotia.

EDWARD VAUGHAN DONGAN.—He was the youngest son of Walter Dongan, of Staten Island, New York. He held the office of lieutenant-colonel of the Third Battalion, and in command thereof at the beginning of that organization. In the skirmish on Staten Island, hereinbefore described, on August 22d, 1777, he was severely wounded and died soon after. He was in his twenty-ninth year at the time of his death, and the record of the times calls him " a young gentleman of uncommon merit, both as a man and a soldier."

ELISHA LAWRENCE.—The family of Lawrence, in Monmouth county, was well represented in the Continental Army and the militia of the State in the Revolutionary War. John Lawrence, however, a land surveyor, was an ardent loyalist, and was imprisoned for his conduct during that period, and his son, Dr. John Lawrence, was arrested and kept in Trenton and then in Morristown, on parole. The Provincial Congress of New Jersey on July 17th, 1776, had an interesting discussion of his case. Another son, Elisha Lawrence, who, in 1775, was sheriff of the county, was one of the most zealous supporters of the Crown. In 1776, at the age of twenty six, he was made the commanding officer of the First Battalion of New Jersey Volunteers, with the rank of lieutenant-colonel, having been very active in organizing the corps. His property was confiscated and sold April 5th, 1779. In the skirmish on Staten Island, August 22d, 1777, he was captured by Colonel Matthias Ogden and the forces under Major-General John Sullivan, and his connection with the Jersey Volunteers ceased at that date. After the war Colonel Lawrence removed to Nova Scotia, retiring on half pay, and he died at Cardigan, Wales, in the year 1811.

JOHN MORRIS.—In the early stages of the war he was commissioned as lieutenant-colonel in the Second Battalion, New Jersey contingent to the Royal army, and he remained in the service until 1780. His services do not appear very prominent, and little is known of him except that on one occasion he chose to disobey the orders of the commanding general of the British Army, who had directed him to destroy some salt factories in Monmouth county. Exercising some conscience in the matter, he spared certain private stores and only levied on public property. The result of this unmilitary conduct is not known to be on record. In the Constitutional Gazette, of August 26th, 1776, he is noted as having been commissioned lieutenant-colonel on the 17th inst. He formerly served in the Forty-seventh Regiment of the British Line.

ABRAHAM VAN BUSKIRK.—He entered the service No-

vember 16th, 1776, with the rank of major, and in 1778 he
was in commission as lieutenant-colonel of the Fourth Battalion. In 1782 and in 1783 he was in command of the
Third Battalion. He distinguished himself, with his battalion, at the attack on Fort Griswold, in the harbour of
New London, Connecticut, and in the massacre which followed, and is spoken of in report by Arnold with applause
for his great services. He did not remain in the United
States after the war, but removed immediately to Shelburne,
Nova Scotia, and became mayor of the city.

MAJORS.

JOHN ANTILL.—Although an officer of this name held the
commission of major in the Second Battalion, New Jersey
Volunteers, in 1778 and 1779, comparatively nothing is
known of his service up to August 15th, 1780, when he was
cashiered for making "false returns and drawing provis-
ions for more men than the effective strength of his battalion." He married the daughter of Alexander Colden,
surveyor-general of New York.

JOHN BARNES.—He was a resident of Trenton, New Jersey, before the war, and was high sheriff of the county of
Hunterdon up to July 18th, 1776, when he was superceded
by the Provincial Congress of New Jersey because he re-
fused to execute the writs issued by its authority. His residence on Queen, now Greene street, below Front, was used
by General Washington on December 29th, 1776, as his
headquarters. In the beginning of the organization of the
Volunteers he accepted the office of major in the First Battalion. He was severely wounded August 22d, 1777, at the

same time Lieutenant-Colonel Dongan was wounded, and died August 31st, 1777, "much lamented as a worthy man and a gallant soldier."

DANIEL ISAAC BROWNE.—There is nothing known of the military record of this officer, except that he held the office of major in the Fourth Battalion in 1778, and left the service that same year. Nor is his personal history known before or after the war.

JOHN COLDEN.—We find an officer of this name as a major in the Second Battalion New Jersey Volunteers in 1778 and 1779. In 1782 we find him, by reason of consolidation of the battalion a captain in the First Battalion. He is believed to be a grandson of Lieutenant-Governor Colden. [See New York Genealogical and Biographical Register, Vol. IV., Jan., 1873, page 171.]

ROBERT DRUMMOND.—Few men did more to make General Skinner's Brigade a numerical success than Robert Drummond. He spent most of the fall of 1776 recruiting for the Volunteers, was very successful and was made major of the Third Battalion November 20th, 1776, and in 1782 and 1783 of the Second Battalion. He was in service during the whole war. A large number of the men enlisted by him fell victims to fever in the Southern campaign. He died in the Chelsea Hospital, district of London, and was buried in St. Luke's churchyard, February 3d, 1789. Major Drummond lived before the war at Acquackanonk Landing, now Passaic, New Jersey, and was a merchant and shipper. He married, April 1st, 1759, Jennie, daughter of Elias Vreeland. A portrait of him is still extant, taken in London in 1784, which represents him in the uniform of a British officer, scarlet coat, blue facings and buff vest.   He was a member of the General Assembly of the Province of New Jersey from 1770 to 1774, a deputy to the Provincial Congress in May, 1775, and again in October, 1775, in January and June, 1776.   On July 2d, 1776, he voted against the adoption of the Constitution of the State. In 1778 his property was all confiscated.   A sketch of the life of this officer may be found in the " Paterson Press " of January 31st, 1877.

THOMAS LEONARD.—This man was one of the first of Jersey tories.   He resided in Freehold, and in April, 1775, the Committee of Inspection proclaimed that he must be treated as a " foe to the rights of America."   We find him as major of the First Battalion in 1778, and leaving the regiment the same year.   After the war he lived in Nova Scotia.

THOMAS MILLIDGE.—Was a resident of Hanover township, Morris county, New Jersey.   He was a deputy surveyor in New Jersey by appointment of the King before the war.   In the course of the numerous surveys he made he acquired a large amount of very valuable real estate. When the war broke out he joined the brigade of loyalists under Skinner—it is thought out of a conscientious regard for his sworn allegiance to the Crown.   He was commissioned major of the Fifth Battalion, December 11th, 1776 ; was made made major of the First Battalion in 1779, and so continued until the end of the war.   All of his land in New Jersey was immediately confiscated by the patriots. At the close of the war he settled in Nova Scotia.   Only

3

once did he return to Morris county, and then his old neighbours gave him distinctly to understand that he was not wanted there. He died in the year 1816. He is always represented as a very honorable man, firm in his convictions of duty and correct in his habits of life.

RICHARD V. STOCKTON.—Major Stockton, of the Sixth Battalion of Volunteers. was a resident of Princeton, and a connection of the patriotic family at " Morven." He, however, was a tory of the most malignant type, and his private character could not have been exemplary, as he was called " Double Dick," on account of sundry unfair transactions. He was also known as the " famous land pilot," because of his skill as a guide in the uninhabited parts of New Jersey. Colonel John Neilson, of the Second Regiment, Middlesex Militia, surprised Major Stockton and his party at Lawrence Island, on the morning of February 18th, 1777, and took sixty-three prisoners. Colonel Neilson was promoted for this little affair to a general officer, and Major Stockton was sent by General Putman in irons to Philadelphia. Washington said of him that he had been " very active and mischievous, but desired that he should be treated as a captured officer, and not as a felon." He was tried August 15th, 1780, by general court-martial for the murder of Derrick Amberman, of Long Island, found guilty and sentenced to suffer death. The sentence seems, however, not to have been inflicted. Some account of his villainous conduct is narrated in Sabine's Loyalists, Vol. II, page 335. After the war he spent the balance of his life at St. John, New Brunswick. He married a daughter of Joseph Hatfield, of Elizabethtown.

Robert Timpany.—He was an Irishman by birth and received his education at the University of Glasgow. He came to America in 1760, lived in Philadelphia several years, and then removed to Bergen county, New Jersey, opening a school at Hackensack. He was made major of the Fourth Battalion in 1778. He was a very ardent soldier during the entire war, always ready to serve his King, and he received several wounds during the campaigns in the South. He attained the great age of one hundred and two years, dying at Yarmouth, Nova Scotia, in 1844. His name on the records is often written Tenpenny.

Philip Van Cortlandt.—He was of the well-known Dutch family of Van Cortlandt, who took such a prominent part among the early settlers of New Amsterdam as land owners on the Hudson river. His birth year is stated as 1739. Although considered a resident of New York, he is found as major of the Third Battalion of New Jersey Volunteers, December 11th, 1776, and he remained in service for all the years of the war. He must be carefully distinguished from his cousin, Colonel (afterwards General) Philip Van Cortlandt, of the Second New York Continental Regiment, or from Colonel Philip Van Cortland, of Essex county, New Jersey, who commanded a battalion and fought on the patriot side under General Heard at the battle of Long Island. The property of Major Van Cortlandt was all confiscated, and he fled to England after the war, dying in May, 1814, aged seventy-four years. In Sabine's Loyalists will be found an account of his own very large family. Four of his five sons were officers in the army of Great Britain.

ADJUTANTS.

JOHN ATCHISON.—An officer by this name was commissioned April 25th, 1782, as an ensign and adjutant of the First Battalion. He had evidently been promoted for service in the ranks. Nothing is known of his history.

GEORGE CYPHER.—On the resignation of Adjutant Thompson, George Cypher was made adjutant of the Second Battalion, September 7th, 1783. This was just at the close of the war.

ISAAC HEDDEN.—He was a lieutenant and adjutant of the Fifth Battalion, commissioned July 29th, 1777, and held the same commission in the First Battalion the next year, but then declined the staff position, and remained in the line until the organization was disbanded. He was made, so Sabine says, clerk of the House of Assembly of the Province of New Brunswick.

PATRICK HENRY.—Mr. Henry was lieutenant and adjutant of the First Battalion until late in the fall of 1778, when he was dropped from said office. His after history is not known.

JOHN HYSLOP.—He was commissioned a lieutenant in the Fourth Battalion, March 25th, 1777, and adjutant of the Third Battalion, June 1st, 1781, and as such remained until peace was declared. His history, or that of his family has not been found.

OZIAS INSLEY.—On August 25th, 1780, he appears as an

ensign in the first battalion and adjutant thereof, but was supplanted by John Atchison as adjutant, in April, 1782. His military service otherwise is not known. With other officers he left for Nova Scotia after the declaration of peace, but died on Staten Island, the scene of his military service.

John Jenkins —On the rolls of the Third Battalion, in 1778, we find the name of this officer as lieutenant and and adjutant, commissioned March 20th, 1777, and he held the line office in the Second Battalion until the end of the war, although John Hyslop takes his place on staff duty in 1781. We find his name after the war as a resident of New Brunswick, Canada, and a grantee of the city of St. John.

Arthur Maddox.—This officer was a captain and adjutant in the Fourth Battalion up to the close of the year 1778, and is then dropped from the rolls and nothing more is known of him.

Thomas T. Pritchard.—He commenced his service as a lieutenant and adjutant of the second battalion at the opening of the contest, and in 1780 is lost to the service.

Cornelius Thompson.—The records show an officer of this name as ensign in the Second Battalion, March 24th, 1777, and as adjutant, commissioned June 29th, 1780. He was promoted a lieutenant, February 22d, 1783, and resigned his commission as adjutant, September 7th, 1783.

Quartermasters.

Fleming Colgan.—He was quartermaster of the Fifth Battalion in 1778, but does not appear in the Volunteers after that date.

Bartholomew Doughty.—This man is enrolled as quartermaster of the First Battalion in 1779.

John Falker was quartermaster of the Third Battalion from its organization until 1781, then transferred to the Second Battalion and resigned February 22d, 1783.

Daniel James.—On the resignation of Quartermaster Falker, Daniel James took his office, and so continued until the Second Battalion was disbanded. He was originally a resident of Philadelphia, but did not return there after the war. It is believed he settled in Shelburne, Nova Scotia.

Thomas Morrison.—He was ensign and quartermaster of the Second Battalion up to the year 1778, was then promoted lieutenant, and still held the office of quartermaster of that organization in 1780.

James Nealson was lieutenant and quartermaster of Lieutenant-Colonel Lawrence's First Battalion in 1778, and afterward a captain-lieutenant for a short time.

William Sorrell entered the service of the King, December 24th, 1776, when he was commissioned quartermaster of the Fourth Battalion. He was also commissioned an ensign and quartermaster of the Third Battalion, July 31st, 1779, and so continued until peace was announced. He was a prisoner of war in Philadelphia, August 28th, 1779, and February 12th, 1780, as is shown by the paroles in the collections of the Historical Society of Pennsylvania.

THEODORE VALLEAU was quartermaster of the First Battalion for a short time after the death of Quartermaster Waddington, in 1782, but does not appear on the rolls the following year.

JOHN WADDINGTON.—During the years 1780, 1781 and a part of 1782, this officer was the quartermaster of the First Battalion, but died of disease during the last-mentioned year.

SURGEONS.

ABSALOM BAINBRIDGE.—Dr. Bainbridge was born at Maidenhead, now Lawrenceville, Mercer county, New Jersey, in the year 1742, graduated at the Princeton College in 1762, and for several years practiced the profession of medicine in his native village. In 1773 he removed to Princeton and was elected president of the State Medical Society. In 1777 he removed to Flatbush, Long Island, and then to New York city, and having accepted protection from the British, he was commissioned surgeon in General Skinner's Brigade, but ceased his connection therewith before April, 1778. He was the great-grandfather of the late Rev. Dr. John Maclean, for many years president of Princeton College, and the father of Commodore William

Bainbridge, of the United States Navy. After service in the volunteers, Dr. Bainbridge resumed his practice in New York and died there, June 23d, 1807.

DANIEL BANCROFT.—He was surgeon of the Second Battalion at the closing days of the war. This is generally considered to be the man who was confined in the prison in Philadelphia in 1777. On being released, he became a more ardent tory than ever before.

HENRY DONGAN.—This officer was surgeon of the Third Battalion up to 1778. He was, no doubt, of the same family as the dead soldier, Lieutenant-Colonel Dongan. His personal history cannot now be ascertained.

CHARLES EARLE.—At the beginning of the war he was surgeon of the Second Battalion, but was dropped in 1781, and on April 24th, 1782, we find him restored to the service, but as surgeon of the First Battalion.

JOHN HAMMELL.—At the beginning of the war we find Dr. Hammell on the patriot side, and July 24th, 1776, he was commissioned surgeon's mate of Colonel Van Cortland's Battalion of Heard's Brigade, New Jersey detached militia. He went with General Heard's command to re-inforce the army at New York, and in his professional capacity took part in the battle of Long Island. Soon after that he professed his allegiance to Great Britain and accepted service in the British Army. He was commissioned surgeon of the Fourth Battalion, New Jersey Volunteers, November 25th, 1776. In the fall of 1777 he was captured on Staten Island by a party of troops under Major-General Philemon

Dickinson, who commanded the New Jersey Militia in the field, and by order of the Council of Safety, November 31st, 1777, he was committed to the jail for high treason. He was surgeon of the Third Battalion at the close of the war.

UZAL JOHNSON.—He was born in Newark, New Jersey, April 17th, 1757. On the 17th of February, 1776, he was commissioned surgeon of the North Battalion, Second Regiment, of Essex County Militia. When the colonies declared themselves independent, he retained his allegiance to the British Crown, and soon after is found in commission as surgeon of the Fifth Battalion of New Jersey Volunteers, afterward transferred to the First Battalion. He went with the New Jersey contingent to South Carolina, and was of great service to the wounded at King's Mountain. He lived in Newark after the war, and died there May 22d, 1827.

WILLIAM PETERSON was surgeon of the First Battalion at the beginning of the war, in the Third in 1779, and in 1782 in the Second Battalion. I am unable to find any other personal record of him than that he was once taken prisoner on Staten Island in 1777.

SURGEON'S MATES.

JAMES BOGGS was surgeon's mate of the Second Battalion during the first two years of the war. He was a Pennsylvanian by birth and residence. He continued after the war as surgeon of the British army in Canada, was made surgeon of the garrison at Halifax, November 22d, 1798, was retired on half-pay in 1814, and died in Halifax in 1832, ninety-one years of age.

———— Haulenbeck.—An officer of this name, with Christian name unknown, is found on the rolls of the Third Battalion of the Volunteers in 1782, but is out of the service in 1783.

Stephen Millidge, a son of Major Millidge, was for several years surgeon's mate of the Fifth Battalion, but he seems to have tired of the medical profession, for, September 14th, 1783, he is found in commission as ensign in the Second Battalion.

Chaplains.

Thomas Barton was born in Ireland in the year 1730. He was educated at Trinity College, Dublin, and in 1752 he came to live in Philadelphia. In 1753 he married in that city the sister of the celebrated David Rittenhouse. In 1755 he received the appointment of a missionary to the counties of York and Cumberland, Pennsylvania. In the year 1758 he became chaplain to the forces under General Forbes after the defeat at Fort Du Quesne. For twenty years thereafter he was rector of the English Church at Lancaster, Pennsylvania. In 1770 he received the degree of Master of Arts from King's College, New York. When the Revolutionary War opened he maintained his allegiance to Great Britain, was forced to abandon his patriotic con- gregation, and removed to New York city in November, 1778. In 1779 he became chaplain of the Third Battalion, New Jersey Volunteers, and died May 25th, 1780, in New

York city, and was interred in the chancel of St. George's Chapel.

DANIEL BATWELL.—He was, October 25th, 1778, commissioned chaplain of the Fourth Battalion, and in the later years of the war he did the same duty in the Third Battalion. He was a resident of Pennsylvania, being rector of Episcopal churches in the counties of York and Cumberland. He was, in 1776, arrested and confined in the prison at York, Pennsylvania, for disloyalty to America. He moved his family into New York, when he joined the Skinner's Greens, and on the declaration of peace went to England.

CHARLES INGLIS was made chaplain of the First Battalion of Volunteers, April 25th, 1781, and so continued until the war closed. In 1783 he moved to Halifax. He was made the first bishop of Nova Scotia on August 12th, 1787, and was thereby the first Colonial Bishop of the Church of England. He died at the age of eighty-two at Halifax, February 24th, 1816. A picture of Dr. Inglis may be found on page 79 of "Lawrence's Incidents in Early History of New Brunswick."

CHARLES MORGAN.—On December 24th, 1780, Charles Morgan was made chaplain of the Second Battalion, but was removed in June, 1783, by the appointment of Mr. Sayre.

JOHN ROWLAND.—At the organization of the Second Battalion this minister took the chaplaincy and remained therein until 1781. The identity of this man with John

Hamilton Rowland, the missionary of Episcopal church in Pennsylvania, cannot now be determined.

JAMES SAYRE.—Mr. Sayre, on June 10th, 1783, took Mr. Morgan's place as chaplain of the Second Battalion. He was a rector of the Episcopal church in Brooklyn, and attended also to his duties with the brigade on Staten Island. Soon after this he removed to St. John, New Brunswick, was a grantee of that city and then accepted a, charge at Newport, Rhode Island. He died at Fairfield, Connecticut, at the age of fifty-three, in the year 1798.

EDWARD WINSLOW was the brigade-chaplain of Skinner's Brigade until the year 1780, when he died in New York, aged fifty-nine. His successor in that office does not appear on the rolls. He was a Boston man, a graduate of Harvard University. He was of the Episcopal denomination and was one time settled in Quincy, Massachusetts. He came to New York city, escaping from the patriotic feeling in his church, and there he formed the friendship of General Skinner, and so joined his forces as stated.

CAPTAINS.

DAVID ALSTON.—He was captain in the Third Battalion in 1778, but resigned the same year.

JOHN BARBARIE.—He was born in the year 1751 and in 1776 organized a company for Skinner's command, commissioned first as a lieutenant and then was made a captain in the First Battalion December 31, 1778. He was captured on Staten Island, in 1777, and lodged in the gaol at Trenton, New Jersey. In 1779 he seems to have been dropped from the rolls, but restored to commission in 1782 and 1783, but in the Second Battalion. He enjoyed the reputation of being a brave and gallant soldier. In the campaign in the South he was twice wounded, once at the siege of Fort Ninety-Six, in South Carolina, May 22d, 1781, and again at the battle of Eutaw Springs, South Carolina, September 8th, 1781. After the declaration of peace he resided at St. John, New Brunswick, and died in the year 1818.

Benjamin Barton.—This officer was a captain in the Fifth Battalion in 1778, but with that year his military service ceased.

Uriah Bleau.—On January 13th, 1777, he was commissioned a captain in the Second Battalion, but the following year he appears as an ensign, first in the Second Battalion and then in the Third Battalion and so continues until the end of the war. In the battle of Eutaw Springs, South Carolina, he was taken prisoner by the forces under General Nathaniel Greene.

Waldron Bleau.—This officer was a resident of the city of New York, but was made captain in the Second Battalion November 23d, 1776, and July 24th, 1781, transferred as captain to the Third Battalion. He was in the volunteers during the whole war. All his property in New York was confiscated, and he died in St. John, that great city of refuge for tories, within a week after his arrival there in 1783.

DANIEL BESSONET was a captain in the Fourth Battalion
until 1779, when he left the service. He belonged to the
family of that name residing in Bristol, Bucks county,
Pennsylvania.

DONALD CAMPBELL was a captain in the Second until
1781 and then captain in the Third Battalion from July
24th, 1781, and so remained until the close of the war.

PATRICK CAMPBELL.—He commenced his service in 1777
as a captain in the Fourth Battalion, in the Third in 1779,
and captain in the Second Battalion in 1781 and 1782.
He left the service on the declaration of peace. He distinguished himself in the Southern campaign, especially at
King's Mountain, where he was severely wounded, and at
the siege of Fort Ninety-Six.

PETER CAMPBELL was a resident of Trenton, New Jersey,
before the war. In a letter addressed by Colonel Joseph
Reed, Washington's adjutant-general, to the Council of
Safety of Pennsylvania, dated January 1st, 1776, (should
be 1777), Pennsylvania Archives, First Series, Vol. V., p.
151, it appears that he was arrested and sent to Philadelphia because he had "been appointed a captain in a new
regiment proposed to be raised for the king's service."
General Washington desired him to be "closely confined."
He was at that time a captain in the Sixth Battalion, having been commissioned as such December 21st, 1776. He
was killed at the fight on Brewton's Hill, near Savannah,
Georgia, December 29th, 1778.

RICHARD CAYFORD.—In the minutes of the Committee of

Safety of the Province of New Jersey, January 12th, 1776, we find a memorial concerning the arrest of this man with two other inhabitants of the county of Cumberland, "convicted of being enemies to this country, by using their influence with the ignorant and unwary to raise a party to oppose the measures adopted for redress of grievances, cursing and ill-treating all Congresses and committees, and refusing to give any reasonable satisfaction for their extraordinary conduct." It was found necessary by the committee to "use spirited exertions for the discouragement of such base behaviour." Cayford was then placed in close confinement, required to pay charges of apprehension and give security for his good behaviour in the sum of fifty pounds. Nevertheless his toryism was too strong for prison bars or legal bonds and he next appears in the following year as a captain in the First Battalion New Jersey Volunteers. He remained in this organization until 1781.

WILLIAM CHANDLER, was the son of the celebrated Episcopal divine, Rev. Thomas B. Chandler, D. D., of Elizabethtown, New Jersey. He was born in May, 1756, and graduated at King's College in the class of 1774. He died in England, October 22d, 1784. He was appointed a captain in the volunteers on Staten Island, April, 1777, but in 1779 he had not received his commission as such. He was considered a tory of the most conspicuous character. A sketch of his father is to be found in Dr. Hatfield's History of Elizabeth, page 537.

JOHN COUGLE.—He was a resident of Pennsylvania in 1775, but in 1776 joined the New Jersey Volunteers and was made a lieutenant in the Fifth Battalion. On July

29th, 1778, he was promoted captain in the First Battalion, and so continued until the close of the war. He died in the province of New Brunswick in 1819, at the age of seventy-three.

DANIEL COZENS was a captain in the Third Battalion of Volunteers December 25th, 1778. He distinguished himself greatly as a zealous officer of the Crown, and in the siege of Savannah, October 9th, 1779, lost his life. For some unexplained reason he appears on the roster of the Second Battalion until the end of the war.

JOSEPH CROWELL was a captain in the Fifth Battalion December 6th, 1776. In 1779 and thereafter he was a captain in the First Battalion. He was a resident of Middletown, Monmouth county, New Jersey, before the war. His property was confiscated and sold March 22d, 1779. He was ordered on one occasion to execute an officer who had never been tried, but so great was the protest against it that the order was countermanded. He removed his family to the province of New Brunswick after the war, and he died there.

EDWARD EARLE.—He was commissioned a lieutenant in the Fourth Battalion November 22d, 1776, and on July 3d, 1781, made captain in the Third Battalion. He served during the whole war, and then moved his family to New Brunswick, and died in that colony.

PATRICK HAGGERTY was commissioned an ensign in the Fifth Battalion in 1776, lieutenant in First Battalion, 1779, and made captain therein December 25th, 1781. He settled in Digby, Nova Scotia, in 1783, and died there soon after.

CHARLES HARRISON was a resident of Trenton, New Jersey, before the war. On the 1st of January, 1777, Adjutant-General Joseph Reed sent him as a prisoner to the Council of Safety of Philadelphia, as one who " had taken a command or appointment as captain in a new regiment proposed to be raised under Isaac Allen for the the King's service." He was a prisoner at York, Pennsylvania, in July, 1778. He must have escaped from this custody, for he served as a captain in the Sixth Battalion of the Volunteers in the fall of 1778, then as captain in the Third, and after 1781 in the Second Battalion. In later years he became a grantee of the city of St. John, New Brunswick.

CORNELIUS HATFIELD, JR.—Few Jerseymen carried their toryism to the extent of this officer. He seemed to have a special hatred to his own townsmen of Elizabethtown. Dr. Hatfield's history of that place has many references to his bad conduct. He was a captain in the volunteers up to the summer of 1778. He was at one time thought to have been a party to the murder of a Mr. Ball, and fled from the country during the latter years of the war. In 1789 he returned to the United States and was arrested for the crime, but escaped punishment by reason of the terms of the treaty of peace of 1783. He died in England at an advanced age.

JOHN HATFIELD was a captain in the Third Battalion in 1778, but does not afterward appear in service. He cannot now be identified with the John Smith Hatfield of Elizabeth Town, New Jersey, who has a very similar record of murder and cruelty, as Cornelius Hatfield, Jr. [See Sabine's Loyalists, Vol. I, p. 524.]

Samuel Heyden was a captain in the Fourth Battalion under Lieutenant-Colonel Van Buskirk. He was captured in February, 1777, gave his parole—which he broke—was taken and sent by Colonel Weeden, of Virginia, adjutant-general of the American Army from Morristown, New Jersey, February 26th, 1777, to the Committee of Safety, with the remark that a "proper attention to him may be found necessary." He seems to have received proper attention, for he does not appear afterward in the service.

Samuel Hudnot, a captain in the Third Battalion until the summer of 1779. Nothing more known of him.

Thomas Hunlock was a captain in the Third Battalion, commissioned December 26th, 1778, but transferred as captain, in 1781, to the Second Battalion, and so remained to the end of the war. He was a half-pay officer on the British lists at New Brunswick after 1783. His place and date of death unknown.

William Hutchinson was a lieutenant in the Fifth, then in the First, then a captain-lieutenant in the First Battalion, April 25th, 1782, and the following year was made captain in the same organization. He was, after the war, a retired half-pay officer of the Crown. He died in Upper Canada.

Garret Keating.—This officer was a captain in the First Battalion in 1777, 1778 and 1779, and then left the service. A man by this name was in the gaol at Trenton, New Jersey, in 1777, and this is believed to have been the same officer.

Joseph Lee.—On the 26th of June, 1776, the Provincial Congress of New Jersey ordered Colonel Abraham Ten Eick, of Somerset county, to arrest him. It was done; and on the 2d of July he was apprehended as a disaffected person and ordered to be confined in the common gaol of Trenton. He was also fined one hundred pounds. He is found, however, soon after this, December 15th, 1776, as a captain in the Sixth Battalion, Skinner's Brigade, warring against the independence of the States. In 1779 he was transferred to the Third Battalion, and in 1781 to the Second, where we find his name, still as captain at the close of the war.

Samuel Leonard.—This officer was a lieutenant in the First Battalion until August 14th, 1781, when he was promoted captain in the same organization. His service extended over the whole term of the war.

John Longstreet was a captain in the First Battalion the first year of the war, but was captured on Staten Island and confined in the gaol at Trenton, New Jersey. He never returned to the service.

Alexander McDonald was a captain in the First Battalion after October 18th, 1782. He died in New Brunswick in 1835, at the age of seventy-two.

Cornelius McLeod was a captain in the Second Battalion until 1780, and then leaves the service.

NORMAN MCLEOD was enrolled as captain of the Second Battalion, January 30th, 1778, but his name, for some reason unknown, is dropped in 1779. But July 24th; 1781, he was re-commissioned as captain in the Third Battalion, and so continued until peace was declared. He evidently belonged to the well-known family of that name in Elizabeth Town, New Jersey.

PETER RUTTAN.—A captain in the Fourth Battalion in 1777, and transferred to the Third Battalion in 1781. The closing year of the war he was not in commission.

SAMUEL RYERSON, of Paterson, New Jersey. He was a captain in the Fourth Battalion, March 25th, 1777, and in 1782 in the Third Battalion. He had a brother Joseph, a lieutenant in the Prince of Wales Volunteers. He took part in the battle of King's Mountain, South Carolina, October 7th, 1780, and was wounded. He lived in Canada after the declaration of peace.

JAMES SHAW commenced his service in the volunteers as captain in the Fifth Battalion, and in the fall of 1778 he was transferred to First Battalion. He was mortally wounded in the battle of Eutaw Springs, South Carolina, September 8th, 1781.

GEORGE STANFORTH.—This officer was captain in the Second Battalion until 1780, and after this date nothing is known of him.

JOHN TAYLOR was born May 15th, 1742, near Amboy, New Jersey. He appears at the close of the war as a captain in the First Battalion, commissioned October 15th, 1780. He was a lieutenant in the same organization from 1776 to date just named. He distinguished himself in the King's Mountain fight. It is quite probable that he was a son of Sheriff John Taylor, of Monmouth county, New Jersey.

Bartholomew Thatcher was confined in Trenton gaol July 2d, 1776, at the same time as Captain Joseph Lee. He became a captain in the Third Battalion of the Volunteers, September 10th, 1778, and after 1780 did the same duty in the Second Battalion.

William Van Allen was commissioned captain in the Fourth Battalion, November 23d, 1776. In 1780 he is found in the same office in the Third Battalion and served until peace was declared.

Jacob Van Buskirk was the son of Lieutenant-Colonel Van Buskirk. He was enrolled at the beginning of the war and was commissioned a captain in the Third Battalion of the New Jersey Volunteers, May 13th, 1780. He was captured in November, 1777, by the troops of General Philemon Dickinson. In the battle of Eutaw Springs, South Carolina, September 8th, 1781, he was severely wounded.

John Williams was a captain in the Fifth Battalion in 1778. He was the officer who, by order of General Skinner, marked houses in Monmouth county with an " R," so that the tories would know who their foes were and whom they were at liberty to annoy.

CAPTAIN-LIEUTENANTS.

JOHN ALSTON was a captain-lieutenant in the Third Battalion until 1779. No particulars of his service, or life afterward, are now known.

JOSEPH CUNLIFF was a lieutenant in 1779, and then captain-lieutenant April 25th, 1782, in the First Battalion until the declaration of peace.

EDWARD STEELE.—This officer was a lieutenant in the Sixth Battalion, May 28th, 1778, in the Third in 1779, then promoted captain-lieutenant in the Second Battalion, and so continued until the close of the war.

LIEUTENANTS.

CHARLES BABBINGTON.—This officer was a lieutenant in the Second Battalion of the Volunteers in 1779.

HENRY BARTON was an ensign in the First Battalion in 1780 and 1781, and promoted lieutenant October 25th, 1782. He remained in service until the end of the war. He was a son of Lieutenant-Colonel Joseph Barton.

JAMES BRITTAIN was born in 1752 and was one of the earliest of Jersey tories. He was very much hated by his neighbours and they did everything to torment and injure him. At last he joined the armed loyalists, with a party of recruits, and was commissioned an ensign in the First Battalion in 1779, and promoted a lieutenant April 25th, 1782. He was considered a brave officer. On one occasion he was taken prisoner and sentenced to death, but he escaped just before the date fixed for his execution and rejoined his command   He died in the year 1838.

William Chew was a lieutenant in the Third Battalion in 1778, and in the Second Battalion until August 15th, 1782, when he was transferred to the Garrison Battalion, with same rank.   He was placed on half pay in 1783, and lived in New Brunswick until his death, in the year 1819, at the age of ninety-four.   His name appears on the army list that year for the last time.

John Coombes was born in 1752; was a lieutenant in the Third Battalion September 10th, 1778, and transferred to the Second Battalion in 1781.   He died in New Brunswick in the year 1827.

Richard Cooper was made an ensign in the Third Battalion in 1781, and a lieutenant in the Third Battalion, October 25th, 1782.

John DeMonzes.—An officer by this name appears in the Second Battalion from 1777 to 1780.   Nothing is known of his service.   Even the spelling of his name is doubtful.

Justus Earle was commissioned an ensign in the Fourth Battalion at the beginning of the war, and promoted a lieutenant in the Third Battalion December 18th, 1781. In August, 1779, he appears as a prisoner of war in Philadelphia, but he was afterwards exchanged and rejoined his command.

JOHN FORD was a lieutenant in the Second Battalion in the the year 1777. He was dismissed from the service in Philadelphia May 3d, 1778, for "conduct unbecoming a gentleman," as we learn from General Clinton's order book.

FRANCIS FRAZER was a lieutenant in the Third Battalion in 1778.

JAMES HARRISON.—A lieutenant in the Third Battalion May 28th, 1778, and in 1780 in the Second Battalion. He remained in service to the end of the war. He fled to St. John, New Brunswick, and was made a grantee of that city.

JOHN HATTON was commissioned a lieutenant in the Sixth Battalion May 28th, 1778. In 1779 he appears in the Third, and in 1780 in the Second Battalion. He never rose to any higher office. He was severely wounded in the siege of Fort Ninety-Six, South Carolina, May 22d, 1781.

ANTHONY HOLLINSHEAD was a lieutenant in the Third Battalion up to January, 1779, when he left the service.

CHRISTOPHER INSLEY.—He started with the Fifth Battalion, but he left the line in 1778.

GEORGE LAMBERT.—He was enrolled January 1st, 1777, commissioned in the Second Battalion in 1779 as a lieutenant, and transferred as such to the Third Battalion July 20th, 1781, and so remained until peace was declared.

JOHN LAWRENCE, an ensign in the First Battalion in 1779, made a lieutenant in the First Battalion, August 25th, 1780, and remained in service the rest of the war. Sheriff John Lawrence, of Monmouth county, New Jersey, had a son John Lawrence, a very distinguished physician, about whom Sabine in his "Loyalists," Vol. II, page 2, gives a long and interesting sketch, and Mr. Salter, in his 'Old Times in Monmouth County," gives a very minute, account, but it is not possible now to identify Doctor Lawrence as this Lieutenant Lawrence. Yet there are many circumstances which make me believe they are the same man.

ENOCH LYON was commissioned a lieutenant in the Third Battalion, September 10th, 1778, but in 1780 was transferred to the Second Battalion and so remained.

DONALD MCPHERSON was a lieutenant in the Fourth Battalion in 1778. He afterwards became a captain in the British Legion.

JAMES MOODY.—He was born in 1744. A farmer before the war, of quiet habits and unpretending life. His loyalty to the King was sincere, and his patriot neighbours exhibited their opinion of him in a most decided manner. This became so annoying that in 1777 he joined the loyal troops of New Jersey, was made an ensign in the First Battalion in 1779, and August 14th, 1781, a lieutenant in the First Battalion. From that moment he became the uncompromising foe of freedom, and "Moody is out," was the cry in any locality in New Jersey which was the scene of antici-

the military service are minutely detailed in "Sabine's Loyalists." On one occasion he attempted the capture of Governor Livingston, and his orders from Lieutenant-General Knyphausen, May 10th, 1780, may be found in "Moore's Diary of the American Revolution," Vol. II, page 307. At another time he was himself taken by General Anthony Wayne, and suffered much cruelty from his captors, but finally broke his guard and escaped. He still continued his attacks upon the patriots, and was often employed as a spy on their movements. Notwithstanding all his years of hardships he was never promoted above a subaltern in the military service. It is difficult to understand now why this was not done. All his property in New Jersey was confiscated. In 1783 a "Narrative of his exertions and sufferings in the cause of government," was published in London, and is believed to have been dictated by him. An interesting and very full sketch of his life will be found in Salter's "Old Times in Old Monmouth." He died in 1809, in Weymouth, Nova Scotia.

JOHN MONRO.—He was a lieutenant in the First Battalion in 1778, but his record is not known.

THOMAS OAKASON.—His service exactly like Lieutenant Monro.

JOSIAH PARKER.—Lieutenant in the Second Battalion December 23d, 1776, and transferred to the Third Battalion July 20th, 1781. He was in commission in the volunteers during the whole war.

ROBERT PETERSON was a lieutenant in the First Battalion the first two years of the war.

JOHN REID.—This officer was a lieutenant in the Fifth Battalion in 1777 and 1778, and in the First Battalion from 1779 to 1783.

MARTIN RYERSON was a lieutenant in the Fourth Battalion until 1780.

JAMES SERVANIER was made a lieutenant in the Fourth Battalion January 2d, 1777, transferred in 1780 to the Third, and remained therein until the end of the war. He died in St. John, New Brunswick, in the year 1803.

DANIEL SHANNON.—A lieutenant in the Fifth Battalion in 1778. Nothing is known of his history.

JOHN SIMONSON.—An ensign in the Fourth Battalion in 1777 and 1778, commissioned a lieutenant in the Third Battalion August 25th, 1780, where he remained until peace was declared, when he removed to the Province of New Brunswick and died there. He was a prisoner of war in Philadelphia in August, 1779.

MICHAEL SMITH was a lieutenant in the Fourth Battalion in 1777 and part of 1778, but is then dropped from the rolls.

WILLIAM STEVENSON.—Commissioned a lieutenant in Second Battalion of the Volunteers December 23d, 1776; native of Monmouth county, New Jersey. A lieutenant in the Third Battalion July 20th, 1781. He distinguished himself in the King's Mountain fight and at siege of Charleston. He died at Weymouth, Nova Scotia, in 1818, at an advanced age.

ANDREW STOCKTON was a lieutenant in the First Battalion at the close of the war. He was probably an enlisted man during the years prior to 1782, and is the soldier who was taken prisoner on Staten Island August 22d, 1777, and confined in the Trenton gaol.

JOHN THOMPSON was made an ensign in the First Battalion in 1777, and a lieutenant in the same organization August 25th, 1780.

JOHN THROCKMORTON.—A lieutenant in the First Battalion the first year of the war. He had the same fate as Lieutenant Stockton ; but, unlike him, did not return to the service.

JOHN TROUP.—A lieutenant in the Third Battalion, Volunteers. He is on the list of those severely wounded at Eutaw Springs, South Carolina, September 8th, 1781.

WILLIAM TURNER.—A lieutenant in the Third Battalion March 20th, 1778. He does not appear on the rolls of 1780–1782, but is found in commission in the Second Battalion at the dissolution of that command.

JOHN VAN BUSKIRK—no doubt a member of the Bergen county family of that name—was made a lieutenant December 7th, 1776, of Lieutenant Colonel Van Buskirk's

Fourth Battalion, and, with him, was transferred to the Third Battalion. Although with this family influence and a service of seven years, he did not advance any in his lineal rank.

William Van Dumont was a lieutenant in the Second Battalion, and July 25th, 1781, was commissioned to the same office in the First Battalion. His service was during the entire war.

John Van Norden.—In 1777 and 1778 an ensign in the Fourth Battalion, and then promoted lieutenant in the Third Battalion, his service ceasing in 1782. After the war he became an instructor in King's College, Nova Scotia, and then removed to Bermuda, where he died.

John Vought.—A lieutenant in the Sixth Battalion, Lieutenant-Colonel Allen, commanding, in 1777 and 1778. His residence before the war was in Monmouth county, New Jersey.

Joseph Waller.—Lieutenant in the Fifth Battalion in 1778. His history unknown.

John Willis commenced his service as ensign of Third Battalion of the volunteers, then made ensign of the Second Battalion, October 24th, 1781, and in 1783 promoted to a lieutenancy.

Samuel Richard Wilson.—A lieutenant in the Second Battalion in 1779. The following year he was transferred to the Royal Garrison Battalion.

ENSIGNS.

JONATHAN ALSTON.—Ensign in the Third Battalion from 1777 to 1780.

PETER ANDERSON, ensign in the Fifth Battalion in 1778. He was a member of Governor Franklin's Board of Associated Loyalists in New York city. He died at the age of ninety-five, in Fredericton, in the Province of New Brunswick.

WILLIAM BANKS, an ensign in the Second Battalion, commissioned October 24th, 1782. He had been a sergeant in that command for several years previous to this date.

JAMES BARTON.—An ensign in the First Battalion August 14th, 1781.

JOSEPH BEAN was an ensign of the Fifth Battalion in 1777 and 1778.

JOSEPH BRITTAIN.—He was a brother of Lieutenant Brittain and had a similar experience as related hereinbefore of that officer. He was an ensign in the First Battalion, October 25th, 1782. He died in the year 183), at the age of seventy-two.

JOHN CAMP.—Ensign in the Third Battalion. Wounded in the thigh at the affair at Egg Harbour, New Jersey, October 15th, 1778, and after that date discharged for disability.

JAMES COLE.—Ensign in the Fourth Battalion in the years 1777, 1778 and 1779, and in August of that year is found as a prisoner of war in Philadelphia. He did not return to the service.

NATHANIEL COOMBES.—Commissioned an ensign in the Third Battalion, May 28th, 1778, transferred in 1780 to Second Battalion, and so remained until the war ended.

EZEKIEL DENNIS.—An ensign of the Fifth Battalion in 1778. His service is not known other than just mentioned.

PETER DUNWORTH.—Ensign in the Third Battalion in 1779.

DANIEL GRANDIN.—This officer was an ensign in the Sixth Battalion for a short time in the year 1778 and then left the service and lived until 1782 in New York. He was on the Board of the Associated Loyalists in that city during the war period, and then lived in Shelburne, Nova Scotia.

REUBEN HANKINSON.—He is first noticed as an enlisted man in the volunteers, when he was taken prisoner on Staten Island in 1777. After he was exchanged he was made an ensign in the First Battalion, August 14th, 1781.

———— HENDORFF was made an ensign in the Third Battalion on February 5th, 1782, and thus remained until the close of the war.

WILLIAM K. HURLET.—An ensign in the Second Battalion in 1778.

JOHN JEWETT was commissioned an ensign in the Third Battalion, July 31st, 1779, and he served as such the rest of the war.

ZENOPHON JEWETT was made an ensign, July 29th, 1778, in the First Battalion, and so remained until 1783.

WILLIAM LAWRENCE was an ensign in the First Battalion until 1780, and then resigned.

JAMES BRAISER LE GRANGE.—An ensign in the Third Battalion in 1777 and 1778, and in the Second Battalion in 1779 and 1780. His subsequent history is not known.

GEORGE LEE.—An ensign in the Second Battalion in 1782 and 1783. His commission bears date December 20th, 1781.

JOHN LEONARD.—Ensign in the Second Battalion December 18th, 1781. He died in 1801 in the Province of New Brunswick.

RICHARD LIPPINCOTT.—This infamous man commenced his military career as an ensign in the First Battalion during the year 1777 and up to the summer of the following year. He then left the New Jersey Volunteers and spent the rest of the war period, with rank as captain, in the direct service of the "Board of Associated Loyalists" in New York city. Captain Lippincott was the officer who hanged Captain Joshua Huddy of the New Jersey State Troops, April 12th, 1782. (See pamphlet by the author of this paper entitled "The Capture of the Block House at Toms River, New Jersey, March 24th, 1782.") After the war Captain Lippincott received from **Great Britain** three thousand acres of land at what is now the city of Toronto, Canada, and a half-pay pension for life. He died in Toronto in the year 1826, aged eighty-two.

RICHARD McGINNIS, ensign in the Third Battalion in 1779. He was killed in the fight at King's Mountain, South Carolina, October 7th, 1780. He was at the time acting as a lieutenant in Ferguson's Corps.

HECTOR McLEAN, ensign in the First Battalion in 1777 and 1778.

COLIN McVANE was an ensign in the Fourth Battalion in 1778 and 1779.

PHINEAS MILLIDGE, ensign in the First Battalion, August 25th, 1780. He was the youngest of four sons of Major Thomas Millidge. He died in Nova Scotia in the year 1836, at the age of seventy-one.

PETER MYER, ensign in the volunteers in the fall of 1778 and 1779. He was killed in a raid in Bergen county, New Jersey, in the year 1779.

JOHN ROBBINS.—Ensign in the First Battalion in 1777 and 1778, and captured on Staten Island August 22d, 1777. He is found in Trenton goal soon after the event.

*RULOFF RULOFFS.—Commissioned an ensign in the Second Battalion October 15th, 1783.

5

STEPHEN RYDER.—An ensign in the Third Battalion December 20th, 1781.

GEORGE RYERSON.—Ensign in the Fourth Battalion in 1778.

JOHN SEAMON.—Commissioned an ensign in the Third Battalion in 1779, but remained in service but one year.

JAMES SERVICE.—An ensign in the Sixth Battalion in 1778.

JOHN SHANNON was commissioned an ensign in the Second Battalion September 10th, 1778, and remained as such until the close of the war.

PHILIP KEARNEY SKINNER.—A resident of Perth Amboy, New Jersey. He was a son of General Skinner. He was commissioned by his father as ensign in the First Battalion November 10th, 1781. He was, after the war, placed in the British line—the Twenty-Third Regiment of Foot—and after various promotions he became, in 1825, lieutenant-general of the British army. The following year, April 9th, 1826, he died in London.

JOHN SWANTON was an ensign in the Third Battalion in 1778 and until 1782, when we find him in the same office in the Second Battalion.

LEWIS THOMPSON was commissioned an ensign in the Second Battalion December 19th, 1781.

Henry Van Allen.—Made an ensign in the Third Battalion December 18th, 1781.

Philip Van Cortlandt, Jr.—Ensign in his father's Battalion, the Third, July 31st, 1779.

Malcom Wilmott.—Ensign in the Third Battalion after October 25th, 1782.

John Woodward, of quaker parentage, living in Monmouth county. But he abjured the faith which is opposed to "warrings and fightings," and we find him as an ensign in the First Battalion August 14th, 1781. He died in the Province of New Brunswick in the year 1805.

Robert Woodward.—Commissioned an ensign in the Third Battalion December 19th, 1781, and remained therein until peace was declared and the New Jersey Volunteers disbanded.

www.ingramcontent.com/pod-product-compliance
Lightning Source LLC
Chambersburg PA
CBHW021520090426
42739CB00007B/700